T0380654

Rosalia Barresi

This
Wellbeing Thing
Recipes for Wellbeing & More

AuthorHouse™ UK
1663 Liberty Drive
Bloomington, IN 47403 USA
www.authorhouse.co.uk
Phone: 0800 047 8203 (Domestic TFN)
+44 1908 723714 (International)

Published by AuthorHouse 07/09/2019

ISBN: 978-1-7283-8969-1 (sc)
ISBN: 978-1-7283-8968-4 (e)

Print information available on the last page.

author HOUSE®

This Wellbeing Thing

I have worked in wellbeing for many years. In different services that have included substance misuse, mental health, autism and learning disabilities. I was part of start-up which involved researching sugar and looking at how it works and how it affects the body. Sugar is bad for us physically and mentally if eaten in large quantities.

The link I began to find was that if we ate foods that support our mental health, we are half way to being well again. I think that we are lucky to have such a wealth of knowledge at our fingertips, but for some it is hard to differentiate that eating certain foods can do something positive to our mental and physical wellbeing. We sometimes need that little bit of help and to be able to source a place where there is a whole array of recipes and nutrient ideas that can give us the help we need.

This book is about just that. I have managed to research thirty recipes that are quick to use and make, but with a twist. They are high in vitamins and minerals that can give us the benefits to support our brain, nervous system and to help prevent depression, anxiety and more. For example; using sunflower seeds and almonds can be beneficial to our brain health by releasing folic acid and magnesium. If we are to eat so much 'modern food' like the processed kind or high sugar refined carbs then we are not able to gain such benefits.

We can be in control of this lifestyle choice if we only know what to do and what to eat. It is so important that we are aware of what we are eating and doing to our bodies.

The Definition of Wellbeing

well-being

/wɛlˈbiːɪŋ/

noun

noun: **wellbeing**

the state of being comfortable, healthy, or happy.

"an improvement in the patient's well-being"

synonyms: welfare, health, good health, happiness, comfort, security, safety, protection, prosperity, profit good, success, fortune, good fortune, advantage, interest, prosperousness, successful

Recipes for Mental Wellbeing:

Using ingredients full of vitamins to help with mental wellbeing

Gram Flour Pancakes

Ingredients

150 grams gram flour
1 egg
Seasoning
2 tbsp sunflower seeds
1 tbsp maca root powder
For topping vegemite and tahini paste

Method

Place all the ingredients into a bowl and mix well. It will make a thick paste and this is normal. Heat up a pan with some rapeseed oil and when hot add half the mixture to make one thick pancake. When browned on both sides remove and add the rest and make the other one. Serve with a spread of vegemite and tahini paste. YUM!

Pancakes made with gram flour, sunflower seeds & maca powder – *gram flour is made from chick peas and is a wonderful source of fibre and protein, maca powder is a root from Peru and gives energy and endurance. Sunflower seeds are rich in omega 3 and 6 EFAs which is fabulous for brain and nervous system.*

Tuna Pasta with Olives, Parsley & Mushroom

Tuna is high in omega 6 EFAs and high in vitamin B1 helpful for poor concentration
Tomatoes Vitamin C which is needed for absorption
Parsley is high in iron

Ingredients

100 grams pasta (gluten free) per person – this makes for two
1 large spring onion thinly sliced
1 large field mushroom chopped
20 grams chopped parsley
2 tbsp rapeseed oil
20 grams green olives sliced in two
50 grams tinned tuna
Seasoning
2 tomatoes chopped

Method

Put a pan of water on to boil for the pasta, meanwhile in a frying pan heat the rapeseed oil and add the spring onions, let them cook for a minute and add the tomatoes. Season well and add the mushrooms. Let them cook for about five minutes and add the tuna.
Cover for about five more minutes and lower the heat.
Add the pasta to the water and wait for this to cook. Take the frying pan mixture off the heat and leave to one side. When the pasta is cooked, drain and add to the pan mixture.
Stir well and add the parsley, olives and season more. Serve and enjoy….

Blackeye bean, Broccoli & Cauliflower Patties with Almond Butter Dressing

Blackeye beans and broccoli are both full of folic acid, high in magnesium which are great for anxiety and depression.
Almond butter – folic acid for anxiety and depression

Ingredients

230 grams tinned blackeye beans
50 grams oats
150 grams cooked cauliflower and broccoli
½ red onion chopped
Seasoning
1 tsp Bouillon stock
2 finger chillies chopped
2 tbsp rapeseed oil

Method

Preheat the oven to 190 degrees. In a food processor place the blackeye beans and the cauli and broccoli, blitz well and then season. Add the chillies, the stock, the onion and the oats. Blitz again and making sure it is mixed well remove, and place into an oven proof dish lined with parchment paper. Cook for about forty minutes.

For the dressing

Ingredients

1 tbsp almond butter
10 grams chopped parsley
Juice half lemon
2 tbsp olive oil

Method

Place all the ingredients in a bowl and mix well. Season if needed.Serve with the patty and enjoy…

Thyme, Spinach & Walnut Pesto

Ingredients

Juice of 1 lemon
30 grams raw walnuts
50 grams fresh spinach
3 cloves garlic
Handful fresh thyme
3 tbsp olive oil
Seasoning

Method

Place all the ingredients into a food processor, blitz until well blended. Taste to make sure the seasoning is right and when ready serve with pasta, cook on a leg of lamb or add to a risotto. YUM!

Walnuts are great for magnesium too and spinach too. Both can help depression.

Avocado Chocolate Slices

Ingredients

1 ripe avocado
3 tbsp sunflower seeds
200 grams mixed raw nuts
6 medjool dates (80 grams)
2 tbsp rice syrup
2 tbsp cocoa powder
1 tbsp rapeseed oil
100 grams dark choc for topping

Method

Place all the ingredients into a food processor, blitz until well mixed, if it sticks then add some water.

Place into a dish lined with parchment and freeze for two hours, then keep in fridge. Slice into squares!

Melt the dark chocolate and smooth over once the slices have set.

Avocado is good for omega 3 and 6 EFAs. Nuts are good for folic acid and magnesium, helpful for anxiety. Dark choc is good for zinc which helps with blank mind.

What does wellbeing mean to you?

Wellbeing is about looking after our physical and mental wellbeing. It is about how we can live our lives and get the right balance from our personal and working life and how we can be more aware of the impact of stress on our lives in order to feel better. It goes on, we are responsible for our wellbeing and therefore asking for help and taking time to give ourselves some selfcare is necessary. Whether it is working in a role that is safe for us, makes us happy and being able to work with people who are tricky but manageable then this can give the right balance. We are surrounded by others all the time, we are noticeably on the edge of stress in this busy modern world and we are on alert quite frequently. With social media and tech taking over our lives, we need to be able to manage our wellbeing as best as possible. Sometimes it isn't so easy to affirm what we need let alone what we want. Being able to make the decisions is a main part of it. We aren't all good at making plans, decisions, being aware and looking after ourselves.

- It is a cliché that comes up very often; we can only be responsible for ourselves unless we have someone who depends on us like a small child, an elderly relative or we work as part of team that helps individuals in a care setting. Empathy is the key. Do you have empathy for others? Or are you solely looking after yourself?

- We are all in this world doing the same thing. We need to be giving ourselves and others the love and support we all need, as well as the planet. Certain things have taken over; social pressure, social media, TV and more. How much does this make you ruminate and how much does it make you feel confident? Do you get a high when you get that like? When someone makes a positive comment? It is very nice to see but how much of it is real? Does it get taken out of context; Facebook and Twitter can be something that is a great thing for work, for our profile in self-promotion, connecting with people and more. If you don't care what people think then great. If you are vulnerable underneath then this is very serious. If we have our own agenda and do what we need to do then we are going to be less disappointed, and much happier. Happiness comes from within and should not be caused by something or someone else. Be happy in you.

Wellbeing can mean anything that creates a better feeling in our lives. Do you have a good healthy diet? Do you exercise? Do you take time to meditate? These are such simple factors that are only a fraction of us are taking part in. The world is a hectic place, it is a scary place and we need to realise how we are all much in the same place.

Wellbeing is about taking responsibility for our care, and to be clear about what you want and that can mean selfcare and selflove.

Self-care is about taking small steps to improve our lives and be happier in ourselves. We need to be able to make the decisions that can help us to be happier. If that means buying a pair of shoes then so be it, or going for some cake then let's do it. As long as we can look after ourselves in the main and be kind to ourselves by eating well, and exercising and being loved.

We have to be able to have some time to ourselves, say no occasionally and be able to reflect on our own time and self. Doing things for ourselves from time to time is important and can make us happier in the long term.

Have a set routine that helps you keep your head and emotions together on a regular basis?

A set routine day in day out is good to help us feel more grounded. It will help us feel settled, and safer. We can really benefit from this if we have a routine most of the time and therefore we can thrive day to day and if lose it, we can get back into it quickly without too much disruption. It is about remembering where you are at. Practicing something like mindfulness, yoga or going to the gym regularly will enable us to keep our energy levels up and be able to sleep better as well as get through the day.

See your friends every week without fail, talk and spend time together so that you know that you are.

Being with people that you care about such as good friends, or members of the family is so important. We can really be there for each other and making time with friends makes our week go easier. Family can be stressful and work too. Everyday tasks are too much sometimes and we need some down time in order to make the harder times easier to cope with. This can all be classed as wellbeing and makes us feel better. We don't have to spend time in expensive restaurants, we don't need to drink too much or go out on a heavy night in order to be able to make ourselves feel better.

WELLBEING has become a real big thing in the last few years. With life being so stressful and difficult for many we are living an overly consuming lifestyle that is hard to take at times. Mental health issues are on the rise, crime is taking over our streets, we are eating more processed food than ever and the pressure to over perform is greater than ever. Let alone the age of social media and tech being upon us.

What can we do the make our lives a little better? How can we support our mind, body and soul in all of this? We can have some control over our lives if we are getting stressed, depressed and anxious. And let's be honest these conditions are on the rise. This section of the book aims to give some insight into such matters and will be able to help with ideas to support your wellbeing with as many areas as possible, from diet (see the recipes) to mental wellbeing, I have worked extensively in this area to complementary therapies and more.

The thirty recipes I have produced are not only healthy but are full of the best nutrients that can support your mental wellbeing. The use of 'real' ingredients is that of logic. If we keep eating rubbish, we will feel like it. The better we eat the better we feel, the more hydrated we are the better we are going to perform as well as feel greater in our minds. Our bodies are 70 percent water and we feel absolutely fantastic when we are not dehydrated. How many of us drink water enough in the day? How many of us 'don't like the taste' of water? This comment makes me laugh so much. It is almost ludicrous. We have been so conditioned to drink sugary drinks or plough our bodies with coffee and tea that for some drinking water is 'alien'.

The power we can give ourselves by putting the right things into our body is so special. We have such an abundance of the right foods etc but many of still don't do it. Many of us are suffering because of it. Why is that? Do we blame food companies? Are we at fault? Is there too much information out there? We need to take responsibility and try to be in control of as much as we can do.

About six years ago after coming out of a very toxic relationship and over consuming a lot, I had studied nutrition on a very scientific basis. I had a huge interest in the subject anyway but I was very naïve about certain matters. The whole sugar v fat thing was confusing. I managed to begin eating certain foods that were low in carbohydrates and I lost some weight and began to feel great. By 2015 when I got involved with the sugar detox program my knowledge on sugar and its toxicity went through the roof. Knowledge is power.

Of course, wellbeing isn't just related to food and nutrition but it can help a great deal with this. It is a good starting point. Mental wellbeing can be linked to food and mood and too much processed/junk food isn't good for mental wellbeing. Depression is one thing and of course there are other interventions that are necessary but a diet high in folic acid and magnesium is beneficial. So, eating plenty of greens and vegetables with these minerals in will help. Food doesn't have to be complicated, it just needs to be understood.

Exercise is the other way forward to working on your mental wellbeing. If we move on a regular basis and this isn't just based on 'going to the gym' 'playing football' or such other. This can mean walking to work, taking those stairs instead of the lift and general everyday movement. If we moved just fifteen minutes per day according to Harvard Health Publishing we can live an extra three years. As long as we get our heart moving we are going to feel better. Our blood moves around and we have less stagnancy. The ten thousand steps per day challenge is a good way to gage movement.

Other forms of wellbeing include spending time with people that make us feel good. We are so busy that we sometimes don't have much time to spend with our greatest friends. The people we love the most, the ones that don't judge us and the ones that understand. Go for a walk with the ones you enjoy spending time with, go and have a meal or cook a meal for them. Go for a walk and more. This is nourishing yourself in the best way possible.

Talk to someone who will listen to you. Talking about our feelings is so powerful that it can help break any difficult emotions we have that will not go away. Talking to someone on a professional level or personal one to somebody you know and trust, will change this dark feeling. This is so vital to one's wellbeing. There are massive numbers of people who cannot talk from fear or shame or just not being able to express themselves because of not being able to as a child. This can be so positive for our wellbeing.

Be there for someone. Step up to the task, selfishness isn't attractive but know your worth. Boundaries are so important, this is so vital for our self-esteem too. We can be so much happier if we know where we stand. Always know your worth, don't let someone take you for granted.

Look after you. Make sure you are getting what you need out of life. Make the right choices for you are made. We can end up making the wrong ones and being in a very difficult situation that isn't helping us at all. Know how much you are worth and be kind to yourself. Allow healing to happen by allowing the feelings to wash over you.

Brown Rice Risotto with Pesto & Broccoli

Ingredients

400 grams whole grain brown rice
1 small sweet potato peeled and chopped
200 grams broccoli chopped
200 grams mushrooms chopped
3 cloves garlic peeled and chopped
1 onion peeled and chopped
1/2 litre chicken stock
125 ml white wine (optional)
Seasoning
30 grams butter

Method

Heat the butter in a pan and add the onion and garlic. Coat the ingredients in the butter and when the onion is browned add the sweet potato and season well. Cook for a couple minutes and add the rice. Add a little stock and stir well. Continue this for about ten minutes and add the wine. Keep stirring so it does not stick. The rice will cook very slowly. Add all the stock and wine until the rice is nearly cooked and add the broccoli and mushrooms. Cover for about five minutes. Season again if needed.

When ready serve with the thyme pesto made below.

Brown rice is ideal every day food with lots of nutrients like Vitamin B6, which can help with every day issues like stress. Brown rice is also good for poor concentration, it is great staple/ carb as is holds a lot of Vitamin B12.

Beans are high in fibre, we need fibre in our bodies every day to be able to function properly and allowing our systems to work.

Miso, Roast Sweet Potato & Mushrooms with Brown Rice

Miso is full of goodness and is high in vitamin K, copper and manganese. Vitamin K is great for regulating calcium levels, metabolises bones and helps to clot red blood cells. Copper is good for forming red blood cells, bone and connective tissue. Manganese is good for our brain and nerve function and to help form red blood cells and our blood calcium absorption.

Ingredients

200 grams brown rice
2 large field mushrooms chopped.
½ red onion chopped
3 cloves garlic chopped.
50 grams kale
1 tbsp miso paste
Seasoning
1 medium sized sweet potato peeled and chopped into small pieces
Olive oil
Two green chillies sliced.

Method

Preheat the oven to 180 degrees. Place the sweet potato onto a baking sheet, drizzle with olive oil and season and put into the oven.
Cook the rice in a saucepan. Approx. cooking time is about ten to fifteen minutes until the water has dissolved. At the end add the kale at the end so it wilts. Take it off the heat and leave to one side for now.
In a frying pan heat up some oil and cook the garlic and onions. Add the mushrooms and the stir well. Season. Add the chillies and stir. Add the miso paste to some hot water and stir well
Add the rice and kale to the mixture and stir in the miso liquid. Cover for a couple of minutes. Remove the sweet potato from the oven.
Take the mixture off the heat and serve in a bowl, sprinkle the sweet potato on top and enjoy!

Miso Hummus

Ingredients

230 grams chick peas
2 tbsp tahini
1 tbsp miso paste
2 tbsp olive oil
Seasoning
Juice half lemon

Method

Place all the ingredients into a food processor and blitz well. Add more oil if needed or some lemon juice. Remove and refrigerate.

Chick peas are good for vitamin B1 which helps us with poor concentration and attention.

Kale & Sunflower Seed pesto

Ingredients

2 tbsp sunflowers
40 grams kale
20 grams rocket
Juice half lemon
Seasoning
3 tbsp olive oil

Method

Blitz all the ingredients in a food processor. Season to taste. Serve with your favourite meat or pasta.

Kale is high in Vitamin C, and fibre and sunflower seeds are high in magnesium, great for depression.

Kale and Sweet Potato Tarts

(Kale high in Vitamin C, needed for absorption for all vitamins and minerals, wound healing and more, sweet potato high in selenium which is a good antioxidant, reduces inflammation and enhances immunity.

Ingredients

Pastry:

180 grams ground almonds

1 egg

2 tbsp rape seed oil

Method

Place the almonds in a bowl and add the oil and mix so it becomes like suet. Add the egg and then mix well then bind it into a ball. Place in the fridge to keep cool for at least two hours.

Ingredients

For the topping:

½ onion
3 cloves garlic
1 small sweet potato peeled and chopped
100 grams mushrooms sliced

100 grams kale
40 grams tomatoes chopped
Seasoning
1 tsp Bouillon stock

Method

Fry the onions and garlic in a frying pan with some rapeseed oil. Add the sweet potato and add the seasoning and the stock. Mix well and add the mushrooms after five minutes. The tomatoes and the kale. Mix well leave covered for further ten minutes on a low heat.

When cooked, leave to one side. Preheat the oven to 180 degrees. Take the pastry out of the fridge and roll out on a flat surface. Cut out four rounds with a cookie cutter and bake in a muffin tin for about ten minutes. When cooked remove from oven and place the filling and cook for further fifteen minutes. Remove and enjoy with a salad.

The A to Z Wellbeing Meaning

A is for Acceptance;

No one is perfect. We are all flawed. We have to be accepted for who we are and accept those who are in our lives. We need to be accepted on a daily basis in work, at home, with friends and in so many more situations. In this day and age with the world being ultra-modern we have the ability to accept people around us.

When it comes to personal relationships acceptance is vital and needs to be something that is inherent in us.

B is for Balance

Balance is important to have in life. Get some balance in your everyday so that you can manage your life. Sometimes we are feeling unbalanced if we take on too much and end up in a really tricky situation we need a good balance between private life and working life.

C is for Communication

Communication is…

A two-way thing…effective communication is vital in any given situation and for your wellbeing. What can happen when we aren't listened to?

We get frustrated…

We get annoyed…

We want to retreat….

We can get riled…

We can become aggressive….

The non-communicator can then react and their behaviour begins to show. Avoidant, ignoring, defensive. They don't know to deal with how you are feeling, so it has to be a negative. Communication is vital in any partnership. Our tone of voice is also imperative or messaging can be seen difficult to read as it is just words. Talking is the best thing and in this day of age of tech, social media and keyboards it is getting harder and harder to communicate effectively. Sometimes it takes a little nudge, a straight up; I need to talk to you and then this can be an invitation to an adult conversation that can be so helpful to a relationship. If someone cannot talk or express how they feel it is a problem. If they clam up or avoid then it is going to be hard to deal with. If someone you love won't open up to you then it isn't going to be easy. If someone is resistant it is going to be a difficult time.

What do you think effective communication is about? Do you prefer someone to shout at you or the avid avoidant?

You choose…

There needs to be a balance; and there needs to be honesty. Being avoided is hard work. It makes you feel unwanted, unloved, unappreciated and underestimated.

Being ignored is like having our ears taped up, we feel misunderstood, and made to feel stupid. We need to be listened to. This is a time to think of ourselves and give ourselves some self-love, self-care and more.

Stop pretending…make your feelings clear no matter how hard it is.

Keep things moving; stop any stagnancy.

Be truthful and be thoughtful to other party,

Clear = Kind

Unclear = Unkind

D is for Dependent

If we are dependent on someone we aren't learning too much. We need to be responsible for ourselves as much as possible. Being dependent on a relationship is one thing, being dependent on a substance is another. Dependency is not something we should be moving towards. It is okay to be dependent for a short time but too long is not going to help us.

E is for Emotions;

Emotions are there and we feel them. Without them we couldn't change how we do things. If we feel an emotion we are sometimes growing and fulfilling our potential. Emotions are sometimes not needed and therefore we are stuck when we get emotional in a situation that is perhaps formal or a work situation. If we have an understanding manager or employer we can be given the space to clear our head and be able to get to grips with our emotions.

This is vital because if we work in a helping role how can we be in work mode?

Work is work and we have to be professional.

But if we don't go through our emotions like grief then it can rear its ugly head later on. Emotions need to be dealt with or we suppress and it will come out later on in the most wrong place.

At times we don't want to sit with our emotions. It is too painful. Why does it make us feel uncomfortable? Thinking too much is also the mistake we can make. Over thinking is like being over tired, it messes with our psyche. Being rational is about getting it out, either writing it down or talking to someone will help immensely. It is about trusting oneself. Do you trust your thoughts and emotions all the time?

That is a hard one; at times we wish to talk to people who know us well. We need that contact and we need that feeling of being able to feel safe.

Emotions are so fragile at times. But if we do not acknowledge them we can melt.

F is for Fun

We need to have fun in our lives. We have to laugh or we will cry. Having fun should be a legal requirement as long as it is good for us and not harming anyone. But at what expense? Be clear what you want and need. Be upfront and be honest.

G is for Gut

Our gut is a replica of our brain. Our gut is governed by our nervous system. The gut is an important factor, if we are not working towards a healthy gut our mind can be in turmoil. Also listen to your gut, there is nothing clearer in this for confirmation.

H is for Happiness

Happiness is important, we need to be happy at least most days. Happiness is a necessary ingredient at least eighty percent of the time in our lives. If we are not happy we can fail to address our real needs in life.

I is for Independent

Be independent, make your own choices and don't be fearful of life. Independence is most important in our lives and we need to be aware of this. Being too dependent is not a positive for us.

J is for Jealousy

Jealousy is hard for both, the one who is jealous and the one who is not. Talk about it and get it out there. Always talk about moving forward from this, don't let it fester. The fact that it is something to do with the past isn't helpful. Trust is needed and respect too.

L is for Love (yourself)

Love you and the ones around you will be loved. Love is so vital for healthy life. Every single one of us needs love in our lives.

M is for Manage

Manage as best as possible. Make some space for your life and give yourself the space to be able to manage as best as you can.

O is for Ownership

Take ownership of your mistakes, your fuck ups and the rest. Be responsible for your own path. Own your mess. Own your issues and the world is a brighter place, don't be ashamed. We are all human and if we learn from our mistakes we can grow.

P is for Positive

Be as positive as you can be, it really does help and it really does make a difference to your life. Being positive is infectious.

Q is for Quandary

Don't get into a quandary, be certain about what you want and what you want to achieve.

R is for Reality

Be realistic in your life, make sure you know what you are getting into. Realism can ground you and keep it all truthful. The truth is always the way forward.

S is for Sustainable

Sustainability is so important in life. Sustained lifestyle is vital in this day and age and needs to be addressed in such turbulent times. If we can live a sustained life we can spread the word and it can be infectious for others.

T is for Talk

Always talk, it helps with the relationships in our lives. Talking is the key to great relationships and partnerships.

U is for Unify

Unify and make time for people. Unify in every way possible, it is such a comfort.

V is for Validation

Self-validation is all we need. No one else has to validate us. We only need to do this for ourselves.

W is for Winning

Win in life, we need to win most of the time and be able to have that feeling that all is going well. A good one to end on.

Sweet Pepper &
Coriander Marinade
Salsa/Salad Dressing

Ingredients

50 grams sweet peppers
20 grams coriander
2 small green chilli
Juice half lemon
2 tbsp olive oil
1 large spring onion
Seasoning

Method

Place all the ingredients into a food processor and blitz for at least thirty seconds. Use as a marinade or as a dressing.

Full of antioxidants, this will sharpen up your taste buds and make any dish taste delicious. Peppers full of vitamin C, chillies are good for pain relief with capsaicin which reduces Substance P, a pain transmitter to your nerves.

Roasted Peppers Stuffed with Feta, Salsa & Sweet Potato

Peppers are packed with vitamin C which is vital in our health as it doesn't store in our bodies.

Ingredients

2 x Romano peppers
2 x small sweet potatoes peeled & cubed
1/2 block feta cheese
1 small red chilli
30 grams rocket
20 grams coriander
Juice half lemon
1 tsp grated lemon zest
2 tbsp rape seed oil
Seasoning

Method

Preheat the oven to about 180 degrees. In an oven proof dish place the sweet potato, drizzle some oil over and season. Bake for about twenty minutes. Meanwhile place all the ingredients aside from the feta and peppers into a food processor and blitz. This will make a delicious salsa, this will make the most of the flavours for this dish. Mash the feta up, and add the salsa to the feta and mix well. Slice open the peppers and deseed.

When the sweet potato is cooked remove from the oven, add these to the salsa and feta. Mix well again. Place the peppers in the dish already used and stuff with the salsa mix. Cook for thirty minutes. Serve; eat on their own or with some fish.

Cashew Cream with Cranberries & Blackberries

Ingredients

140 grams raw cashews (soaked overnight in water)
Half cup almond milk
100 grams dried cranberries & blackberries (soaked in hot water for 10 minutes)
2 tbsp flaked almonds

Method

When the cashews have been soaking for at least twelve hours, drain them off and place into a food processor. Blitz for about three minutes and add some almond milk to make smooth. Add more almond milk if you need to.

Drain the fruit and place in the food processor and blitz until mixed well. Remove and place into a bowl. Take some small glass bowls and spoon in two to three tablespoons of the cashew cream and then spoon the fruit on top. Sprinkle the flaked almonds and refrigerate for two hours. Serve and enjoy.

Sunflower Seed and Miso Dressing/Marinade

Ingredients

2 tbsp sunflower seeds
2 tbsp rapeseed oil
1 tsp miso paste
4 sage leaves
Juice half lemon
Seasoning

Method

Place all the ingredients in a processor and blitz, use as a marinade with salmon or chicken or a dressing.

Sunflower seeds are full of magnesium that can combat depression

Thoroughly Beetroot Chocolate Cake

The colour of beetroot shows level of goodness in such a plant. High in antioxidants and good for energy as well as supportive to brain and digestive health. It is also a great food for athletes. It helps also to keep blood pressure at a good level.

Ingredients

500 grams beetroot
100 grams butter
50 grams soft brown sugar
2 tbsp date syrup
1 tbsp vanilla essence
1 tsp baking powder
150 grams ground almonds
3 eggs
2 tbsp cocoa powder
2 tbsp rapeseed oil

Method

Line a cake tin with removable bottom with parchment paper. Preheat the oven to 200 degrees.

Cream the butter, and add the sugar and stir well. Add the vanilla essence, the baking powder and the cocoa powder, mix thoroughly with a wooden spoon before adding the almonds. Add the oil and make sure it is stirred well. Add the eggs and stir well and add the beetroot. Making sure the mixture is really stirred well. Pour into the cake tin and place in the oven for about forty-five minutes. It may need bit longer but check it is cook with the knife test. It is a soft cake so wait until cooled down, or eat warm.

Broad Bean Pate

Ingredients

150 grams cooked broad beans
1 large spring onion
2 tbsp tahini paste
Seasoning
Few sprigs rosemary
1 clove garlic

Method

Place all the ingredients into a food processor and blitz for about a minute. Add more season if needed. Spread on toast or have with vegetables as a starter.

Broad beans are so full of goodness, high in fibre and a wonderful veg to eat when it is in season; June. They can help with Parkinson's disease as well as the brain and keep bone healthy. They can help with anaemia and high blood pressure. They have a high concentration of thiamine, vitamin K, vitamin B-6, potassium, copper, selenium, zinc and magnesium.

Pistachio Encrusted Salmon

Ingredients

50 grams shelled raw pistachios
10 grams flat leaf parsley
1 clove garlic
2 tbsp olive oil
Seasoning
2 Salmon fillets

Method

Place all the ingredients into a food processor or nutri-bullet and blitz for about one minute. Place in a container in fridge if not using straight away or spread over a salmon fillet and bake for about 10 minutes in a hot oven. Serve with some green veg.

Salmon is a wonderful brain food and is so full of omega 3 and 6, essential fatty acids. Pistachios are good for high blood pressure, as well as lowering cholesterol, great of gut bacteria, they are high in antioxidants and can benefit your blood vessels.

Feta, Red Onion & Fig Tart

Figs are so good for your digestion, they can help keep all moving and the gut is linked the to the brain. If we keep the gut moving our body works better.

Ingredients

For the pastry;
!50 grams ground almonds
2 tbsp rapeseed oil
1 egg

Method

Place the ground almonds into a large bowl, add the oil and stir well. Add the egg and mix with a spoon and eventually bind together with your hand. Wrap in cling film and leave in fridge for two hours. Preheat the oven to 180 degrees. When chilled, roll the pastry in the cling film with rolling pin and use a large cookie cutter to cut into four rounds. Place in a muffin tin and bake for about ten mins.

Ingredients

For the topping;
1 medium red onion chopped
100 grams dried figs
100 grams feta cheese
Seasoning
Oil for frying.

Method

Place a frying pan on low heat and add some rapeseed oil, add the onions and cook for five minutes. Add the figs and cook on low heat until slightly caramelised. Leave to one side.
When the pastry is part cooked put the onion/fig mixture into the rounds and cook for further ten minutes. Remove from oven and add the feta. Cook for another five minutes, remove and serve on bed of salad. Yum!

Wellbeing Interventions That Can Increase Our Health & Wellbeing

Acupuncture; this amazing Chinese therapy is somewhat a mystery but works. It works on the qi or energy lines that are tweaked by inserted needles and these release any blockages or disruptions. It can work for many ailments physical, emotionally or mentally. Some to mention are skin conditions, joint pain, headaches, respiratory or digestive. I have had some really amazing results such as curing tennis elbow, tarsal bone pain, misaligned joints and more. I feel well pretty much most of the time and this I believe is to do with having acupuncture on a regular basis.

Ear acupuncture; an amazing treatment that has been used in substance misuse for many years and calms the brain and relaxes the body. Working on the same principles as TCM tt can bring a sense of zen to the body enabling stress to be relieved from the brain. It is great for other addictions such as smoking and I have had results with sugar addiction too.

Exercise; Moving is what makes us work better. We can become stagnant when we don't move. I am not just referring to the gym, but walking when we can, getting up from desks at every opportunity, taking the stairs and carrying bags. We need to move frequently. Our muscles depend on it.

Massage; this is the king of wellbeing. The touch element helps to reduce tension, eases pain and enables us to feel better instantly. It is something that is passed onto generations in Asia (like Indian Head massage), to take care of the hair and to help reduce tension in the way of pressure points being eased.

Reflexology; an ancient treatment based on Chinese medicine that rebalances and boosts our immunity. It works on the qi, which ends at the feet and with the body mapped out on the sole of the foot, also works on hand and face too.

Reiki; energy healing by the master or healer that channels it into the receiver's body. It is calming and grounding. This can be highly emotional but can settle us beautifully.

Shiatsu; very similar to acupuncture, and a Japanese therapy but done on a futon and using pressure from the hands and thumbs it works on the qi and clears blockages and it ultimately relaxing.

Talking Therapies; It's good to talk! Talking is about re-evaluating the way we look at ourselves. It also makes us think how we reflect on our lives. Talking to a professional can be so therapeutic for our psyche. Unless we can get something out of our head if it will not shift then talking is a positive thing.

Yoga; get those chakras opened, our seven chakras are linked to all parts of the body, mind and soul. It works on the breath, meditation and body positions and is a Hindu and spiritual discipline.

Pistachio Roasted Beetroot

Ingredients

500 grams beetroot
50 grams shelled raw pistachios
10 grams flat leaf parsley
1 clove garlic
2 tbsp olive oil
Seasoning
2 cloves garlic
Oil for drizzling

Method

Preheat oven to 200 degrees. Peel and chop the beetroot and place in an oven proof dish. Blend the other ingredients in a food processor and form into a paste. Add to the beetroot and cook in the oven for forty-five minutes. Make sure it is cooked through and serve with your favourite protein.

The colour of beetroot shows level of goodness in such a plant. High in antioxidants and good for energy as well as supportive to brain and digestive health. It is also a great food for athletes. It helps also to keep blood pressure at a good level.

Beetroot & Feta Bregg

The colour of beetroot shows level of goodness in such a plant. High in antioxidants and good for energy as well as supportive to brain and digestive health. It is also a great food for athletes. It helps also to keep blood pressure at a good level. Feta cheese is made from sheep's milk, its high amount of B vitamins, phosphorus and calcium. So ideal for our bones and keeping us strong. To be physically strong is as important as mentally strong. It should however be eaten in small quantities as it has higher sodium.

Ingredients

150 grams ground almonds
150 grams chopped cooked beetroot
100 grams feta
2 garlic cloves chopped
1 tsp baking soda
Splash water
2 eggs
Seasoning

Method

Preheat the oven to 180 degrees. In a large bowl mix the ground almonds with the baking powder and the water, add the seasoning. Add the beetroot, garlic and the feta, mix well. Add the eggs mix again and place in a lined loaf tin. Bake for approximately forty minutes. When cooked place a knife in it to see if it comes out clear. If so, leave to cool or serve hot with butter.

Chorizo & Flageolet Beans in Passata

Flageolet beans are full of fibre, they keep your system healthy and also are full of potassium, magnesium, iron, manganese, copper and vitamin B9. Tomatoes are filled with lycopene which is beneficial for fighting cancer.

Ingredients

230 grams flageolet beans
1 onion chopped
3 cloves garlic chopped
20 grams butter for cooking
1 tbsp Bouillon stock
Seasoning
1 tsp fennel seeds
100 grams chopped Chorizo

Method

Heat the butter in a pan, add the onions and garlic. Add the seasoning, the stock and the fennel seeds then add the chorizo. Cook for about ten minutes on a moderate heat. The juices from the chorizo will begin to ooze and add real flavour. Add the beans and stir well, followed by the passata. Stir well and leave on low heat to cook for thirty minutes. Check on it after a stir well, season if needed and leave for further ten minutes. Take off heat and serve with rice.

Tapenade Chicken

Chicken is high in protein and high in tryptophan. It is ideal for depression as it is an essential amino acid that is a precursor to the neurotransmitter serotonin. It replaces serotonin to help with mood. Serotonin can be depleted with some illnesses like depression so serotonin can really help. Olives are a high fat plant food that contain good amounts of vitamin E which works as a wonderful antioxidant. Black olives are a high source of iron.

They also contain high amounts of copper and calcium, two minerals that are needed in the body.

Ingredients

4 chicken legs
4 garlic cloves chopped
1 small onion chopped
20 grams parsley
2 tbsp olive oil
150 grams green olives pitted
Seasoning

Method

Place the olives, garlic, onion, parsley and oil in a food processor. Season well. Place the chicken in a flat dish and cover with the marinade. Cover and leave in fridge for an hour. Remove after this time and preheat the oven to 160 degrees. Cook covered in foil for about forty minutes to an hour, until the chicken is cooked through. Remove the foil and place in oven again for ten more minutes. Serve with your favourite vegetables.

Chicken Pizzaiola

Ingredients

4 Chicken legs
250 grams sweet potatoes
4 cloves garlic
500 grams tomato passata
20 grams fresh oregano
1 tbsp olive oil
Seasoning

Method

Preheat the oven to 180 degrees, preparing an oven dish. Peel and slice the sweet potatoes, leaving them quite chunky, place them in the dish.

Lay the chicken legs on top or next to the sweet potatoes. Slice the onion and garlic and mix this in with the sweet potatoes and chicken too. Pour over the passata and oil and mix well. Season well and add the oregano chopped, sprinkling over the top. Place in the oven and cook for about an hour. Or until the chicken is cooked through and browned. Add more seasoning if needed.

Chicken is high in protein and high in tryptophan. It is ideal for depression as it is an essential amino acid that is a precursor to the neurotransmitter serotonin. It replaces serotonin to help with mood. Serotonin can be depleted with some illnesses like depression so serotonin can really help. Sweet potatoes are high in antioxidants, their colour shows this. They are high in beta-carotene, vitamin C, and magnesium. They can reduce inflammation too.

Salmon & Pine Nut Salad

Salmon is full of goodness in EFAs, omega 3 & 6. It is great for the brain and the neurological system.

Ingredients

2 x Salmon fillets
1 yellow pepper
40 grams rocket leaves
12 cherry tomatoes
1 courgette

For the dressing

1 tbsp tahini paste
2 tbsp olive oil
Juice half lemon
Seasoning

Method

Slice the pepper and grill it until soft and brown. Season the salmon and grill as well until cooked, may only take about three minutes per side. You may want to cook it for longer. Take a frying pan and place on the heat for couple minutes when it's hot throw in the pine nuts into the pan to toast. Place the rocket leaves into a serving bowl, strip the courgettes with a peeler to create ribbons and add to the rocket. Cut the tomatoes and add these too. Take the pine nuts off the heat. Lay the peppers on the salad then place the salmon on top. Scatter the pine nuts. Mix the dressing ingredients in a small bowl and drizzle over the salmon salad. Enjoy!

Prawn & Chilli Courgetti

Ingredients

200 grams peeled prawns
1 large courgette
1 large red chilli
2 tbsp olive oil
2 cloves garlic
Seasoning
Juice half lemon

Method

In a pan fry the garlic and chilli and season well. Spiralise the courgette or if you can't do this then use a peeler and form ribbons. Add the prawns to the garlic and chilli, squeeze the lemon and mix well. Add the spiralized courgette and mix well. Season again if needed and serve.

Prawns are healthy as they contain magnesium, which plays a role in bone development and nerve and muscle function. This can really help with depression. Chilli is also a fantastic analgesic for us and we can gain a lot of benefits from having chilli in our food for our physical health.

Blueberry & Oat Breakfast

Ingredients

50 grams blueberries
30 grams raspberries
50 grams oats
30 mils oat milk
30 grams natural yoghurt
Pinch cinnamon

Method

Soak the oats for up to one hour beforehand (or overnight) in the oat milk, add the cinnamon. When they have been soaking place them in a bowl add the fruit, leaving some blueberries for decoration. Mix well, then add the yoghurt and serve in a glass. Place the blueberries on the top. Eat for breakfast or for a dessert!

Blueberries are a great source of antioxidant, they are also one of the best fruits for us. The colour depicts this. Oats are a fabulous way to start the day, full of goodness, slow releasing carbs and natural yoghurt is a great source of protein.

Cheese & Fennel Grilled Frittata

Ingredients

3 eggs
50 grams goat's cheese chopped.
1 small onion chopped
2 cloves garlic chopped
Half fennel bulb thinly sliced
Seasoning
1 tsp Bouillon stock
Rapeseed oil for frying

Method

Fry the onion and garlic in a pan. Beat the eggs in a bowl and season well, leave to one side. Add the fennel to the garlic and onions, season well and add the stock too. When cooked add to the eggs, along with the cheese and mix well. Preheat the oven to 160 degrees, grease a muffin tin and place the mixture into about four or five of them. Bake in the oven for about 30 minutes or until cooked through and browned on top. Serve with smoked salmon and raw fennel slices.

Eggs are good for omega 3 & 6; essential fatty acids can help our nervous system as well as our brains. Fennel is high in potassium and it tastes delicious.

Salmon Salad

Ingredients

2 salmon fillets
1 celery stick chopped
50 grams baby spinach chopped
1 beef tomato chopped
30 grams cucumber sliced
Seasoning
2 tbsp rapeseed oil
Juice half lemon

Method

Heat the oil in a pan and cook the salmon aiming for about 3 minutes on each side. Season the salmon and in a large bowl arrange the spinach and other vegetables, drizzle the leftover oil on the top, season and squeeze the lemon on too. When the salmon is cooked then flake it over the top of the salad.

Salmon is full of EFAs omega 3 & 6, good for our brain and nervous system. Spinach holds a lot of iron and this is good for our bones, blood and also contains vitamin C.

Risotto with Green Beans, Feta & Pesto

Whatever beans you use, they are nutritious and delicious. They can help our digestive system hugely and are full of protein, so if you don't want to eat lots of meat then it is a good way to pack in the protein. Green beans, are a rich source of vitamins A, C, and K, and of folic acid and fibre. They also contain high amounts of magnesium and folic acid.

Ingredients

400 grams risotto rice
1 small sweet potato peeled and chopped
200 grams green beans trimmed and chopped
200 grams fresh spinach roughly chopped
3 cloves garlic peeled and chopped
1 onion peeled and chopped
1/2 litre chicken stock
125 ml white wine (optional)
Seasoning
30 grams butter

Method

Heat the butter in a pan and add the onion and garlic. Coat the ingredients in the butter and when the onion is browned add the sweet potato and season well. Cook for a couple minutes and add the rice. Add a little stock and stir well. Continue this for about ten minutes and add the wine. Keep stirring so it does not stick. The rice will cook very slowly. Add all the stock and wine until the rice is nearly cooked and add the beans and spinach. Cover for about five minutes. Season again if needed.

When ready serve with the thyme pesto made below, and feta cheese. YUMMY!

Cauliflower Steak with Pistachio & Sunflower Seed Sauce

Cauliflower has many nutrients and it appears to be used more and more these days. It is used instead of carbs which can stop our insulin levels from spiking therefore keeping our blood sugar levels stable. It also is a real beneficial food full of vitamin C, vitamin B6, folate and potassium. Pistachio nuts are so nutritious too, with one ounce containing more potassium than half of a large banana, they are high in protein, fibre and antioxidants too.

Ingredients

Half cauliflower sliced into steaks
50 grams pistachio nuts
50 grams sunflower seeds
Seasoning
1 tsp paprika
30 grams parsley
2 cloves garlic chopped
2 tbsp rapeseed oil for cooking
A splash soy sauce
1 tbsp almond butter

Method

Preheat the oven to 180 degrees, place two to three steaks on a baking sheet and drizzle with some of the oil and season. Place in oven for about thirty minutes.

Meanwhile blitz the nuts and seeds in a food processor, heat some oil in a frying pan and place the ground nuts and seeds in the oil. Season and add the paprika, leave on a low heat for few minutes. Add the almond butter and the soy sauce, mixing well all the time. It will be slightly sticky add some more oil if it gets too sticky. Chop the parsley and add mixing well. Take the cauliflower out of the oven when it is cooked, and place the sauce over the top and serve. YUM!

Printed in the United States
By Bookmasters